CREATING NEW INDIA

LET'S RE-WRITE THE INDIAN POLITICS

AN IMAGINATION BY
RAGHAVENDRAN RAO

Copyright © An Imagination By Raghavendran Rao
All Rights Reserved.

Dedication

This book is dedicated to all those Indian living in India or in any other country

Contents

Contents

Foreword

This book is written based on my imagination and not to hurt any individual or any Political Party. I have been watching the country since my childhood and travelled to different parts of India.

Though there are developments happening around and still I am not convinced that whether we are really living in a developing or developed country compared to other countries.!

What all comes to my mind is like a dream, I am trying to pen down here and expect everyone to read and appreciate my thoughts if you like it. It's all my imagination, I shall be happy if it comes true.

My sincere thanks to all those Freedom Fighters and those who were or are running the country so far. I also salute each and everyone who has rendered their services to the nation in some way or other.

Acknowledgements

I am thankful to all those who were directly or indirectly part of this book writing.

First of all thanks to my family members, friends, mentors, online webinar hosts, online sales partners and most importantly the Politician who forced me to think and write a book on re-writing the Politics.

I may not be doing justice if I do not thank my readers, who will support me through their valued comments on the review section.

Thank you all...

About The Author

I am Raghavendran Rao known as "Raghu", my family and friends call me "Sudhakar" born and brought up in a small village "Pudukkudi" in Mannargudi Taluk, Then, Tanjore District (Currently Thiruvarur District) in Tamil Nadu, India. After Schooling moved to New Delhi to find Bread & Butter for life, then settled there itself, working in private organizations like Films, Advertising and Information Technology. subsequently got into my own business. Finally, I have decided to write a book in a very simple language, so that it reaches everyone.

The idea of "Creating New India" is to make India, the most powerful country in the world.

I am pretty confident that it is possible if the voters believe in this and convert my imagination into reality. Request everyone to read this book, in order to understand that we not only Make-in-India, but we also have to make "India"

Raghavendran Rao

Son of Smt. Kantha Bai & Late Sri C N Vasudeva Rao

Independent, Autonomous Body

No Govt post after retirement to CBI ED, JUDGES etc., They have to follow rules & work for what is right without favouring any individual or party.

All these departments will be given free hand to work and shall not allow pressure from any individual or party forcing them to take any steps in favour of anyone or in their connection.

Also, employees or retired employees of these departments will never be given any post like Governor, President of India, High Commissioner etc.,

Of course, they can be a member of Advisors of their respective departments, in order to utilize their experience. However, only honest and sincere candidates will be given preference.

Courts

Verdicts of lower courts are being pronounced differently by higher Courts and judgements go in favour of particular people on various occasions, which should not happen unless there is solid evidence to do so. If done by any higher court, then seriously look into the inefficiency of the concerned Judge of the lower court for the wrong judgment and take necessary action.

CHAPTER THREE

Election Commission of India

EVM will be tested by Private IT companies before voting starts. Once voting is completed, within two hours, counting will start and results will be announced, Thereby curtailing huge expenses being incurred now on safeguarding & security provided etc., thereby avoiding doubts on any party and ensuring conducting a fair election process.

Find out a way to use technology for the ONE DAY VOTING system instead of phase-wise voting on different dates. Do not drag for days...and no more gap between voting & counting to have fair elections. If possible, we may go for online voting through mobile phones too.

Cancel his/her nomination, If found paying a bribe or of any kind to people for the vote and also be banned for a lifetime to contest any election in India. This will be applicable to their whole family members. If one is guilty all the family members will be punished accordingly. One person one term basis elections. He or She including their family members may not be given a second chance to contest any election and allow others to do so.

Freebies if any announced by any Party shall be considered as "Bribe"

CHAPTER FOUR

Agriculture

Due to a lot of "Bribes" being provided to voters in the name of "Freebies" are making common men handicapped and since they are getting the necessary things for free, they become lazy resulting which their next generation will suffer like anything. Neither will they be able to spend on their studies nor will they become hard workers. Thus, after a few years, I am afraid of what will happen to agriculture.

Also, the Government has to support (Kisan) Farmers and help them in every step so that committing suicide reduces to "zero".

Encourage even youngsters to get into agriculture and natural farming etc., thereby ensuring that our country produces maximum eatables and exports to other countries to earn foreign currency.

Will focus on natural farming, even every village, people would be asked to produce any item/s according to the location/soil etc.,

Always be ready to face any national calamity like Rain, Flood, Tsunami, Earthquake, or terrorist attack etc.,

Create district-level awareness campaigns about the schemes announced by the Government and help them to avail.

Those who are from a village and working in Metro cities or in other countries, instead of investing your money into Fraud Investment companies or any other schemes, where at the end of the day you have to face "Loss", better to invest in your village to promote Farmers and focus on Agriculture and set up Solar-Agro Projects.

Offer Tractor on rental and charge electricity generated from Solar Project.

Farmers should come together and set up a commercial business to undertake the processing of farm products and retailing of those products.

ABOVE ALL ACCORDING TO ME, A FARMER (KISAN) HAS TO RUN THE AGRICULTURAL MINISTRY INSTEAD OF ANY "KURTA WALA" NETA WHO DOES NOT KNOW THE GROUND REALITY.

CHAPTER FIVE

Art & Culture

We have different Language speaking people and adopting different cultures that too which are there from many years and most the tradition, culture and festivals are shrinking day by day and the younger generation are not even aware of various things and in order to retain the culture, tradition, Government has to set up various cultural centres where we can teach the next generation, also through the medium of the Internet.

Government should recognize and reward those who adopt our culture and work for the same.

CHAPTER SIX

Commerce & Industry

Enter Caption

India has missed the industrial revolution as it was under British occupation.

Post-independence we missed industrialization and jumped right into the service sector. Because of this, we lack manufacturing skills and people hate labour-intensive jobs and prefer to work in an air-conditioned office. Excessive concentration of jobs in the service sector is a great concern.

Even our neighbouring country's manufacturing hub is facing the challenge of people preferring services over blue-collar jobs, hence forcing people to work in factories.

We too encourage people to work in industries and manufacturing units, thereby can take production to a great height.

Setup at least One Industry in each District (minimum) and employ 60% of employees from the same district to give employment opportunities to youngsters and elders who want to stay with their families in a nearby location. Better, our Government itself set up some industries.

Give Tax holidays to those who set up Industries in Rural Areas and employ 60% from the local area, to create employment opportunities while developing the Rural economy simultaneously.

Look at what we import and then try to manufacture them and similarly look for all export opportunities and export as much as we can, to generate more revenue.

CHAPTER SEVEN

Communication & Infotech

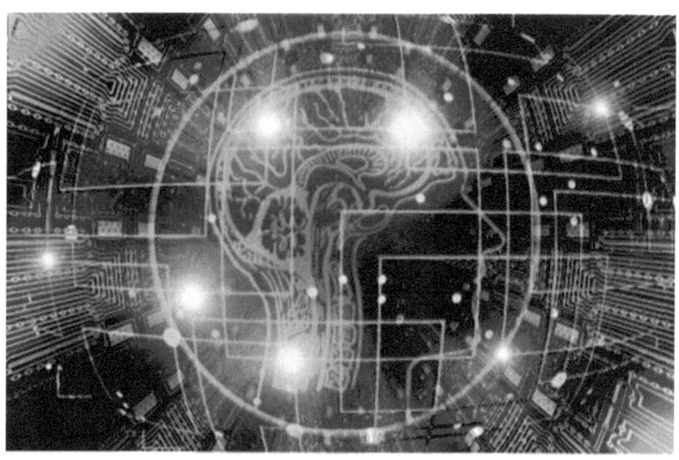

Invite Indian companies to become something like Google, Microsoft, Intel etc., and help them to grow, thus more employment opportunities can be created and generate revenue from all other countries.

Also the Mid and Small size IT companies can be attached to the leading companies as vendors officially and sub-contract as much as possible, so that they also grow along with and they too can create more employment opportunities at their level.

A senior person from an IT & Telecom company will be the IT & communication Minister.

Defence

A person who worked in Defence has to become a Defence Minister. Only honest and clean people in his / her career shall be considered for the post.

Manufacture weapons and defence related items in India itself.

Majority of the staff working in defence do not have full-time job allocated to them,, unless there is a threat from other country or War etc., In order to keep them busy, we can have our own manufacturing units in various locations, where weapons or related products can be manufactured which will save cost on import.

No more tax exemption on any product to anyone in the country as everyone is being paid for the job assigned to them. Thereby we can save more on GST etc.,

CHAPTER NINE

Education

Only one central board for conducting examinations of 10 and 12th and not state-level for every state. Let's maintain uniformity in the education system.

change the system, study based on the interest of the student and allow them to specialize in the subject where he or she has to take up a career.

Summer vacation is meant to relax from educational activities and normally children do not enjoy nor can plan any holiday trip with parents at least once a year. Even if they go out they have to complete their "Home Work" which is a burden for them. Children also need rest from mental stress. No more holiday home work on summer vacation.

Many subjects where students spend a lot of time studying are NOT AT ALL USED for the rest of their life. Hence we need to minimize the number of subjects and focus only on those in which they are interested so that they can put more effort into the subject which will be useful for them to decide on their career.

There are subjects like History, Geography etc., are not essential, just an overview will do and they can always refer internet as and when required.

Almost in every class up to 12th, students were asked to prepare charts, Drawings etc., though they don't want to become an ARTIST OR PAINTER, still, spend time on this instead of focusing on their preferred subject. These Need to be changed.

Politicians' son/daughter relatives have to study in Govt schools and colleges in their constituency itself. They are not supposed to send them overseas for better study, as we do not have an education system in a proper way. Once this is done, they will make our education system better.

Need to change the present system of education and ensure that based on the Student's interests they will be taught, so that the younger generation gets a job of their choice. Mostly everyone studies the same subjects and is placed in different segments. They are forced to learn many things which are not part of their career and never ever used in their lifetime. Also, learn new things after joining a job which is relevant to their career.

Best Indian Brains/Scientists are working abroad whereas we do not provide them facilities to work in our country. Let's give them all assistance to utilize their intelligence for the growth of our country

Government can start Online Schools (Like open schools, and universities) with very low fees for students to join from anywhere in the country to get the best education online which will reduce pollution when they avoid transportation and also save a lot of mishappenings, particularly for Girl students.

Even physical education & training can be made online, through which students can assemble in their local areas at different locations/cities and Trainers can train them online from one place.

CHAPTER TEN

Employment

Will convert many businesses like Insurance etc., to Govt from Pvt and employment shall be given to youngsters. Excess profit money goes to private companies now, which Govt can accumulate spend for development.

More Government businesses like Telecom, Airways, Railways etc., shall be introduced and provide more employment to the unemployed.

Identify one person from each family to provide employment or assist them to become an entrepreneur, who in turn may give employment opportunities to many others.

Set up Small scale industries in every village and excess production can fetch revenue through exports to other countries.

No need to register with the employment exchange or prepare and write exams.

Interviews can be conducted that too based on marks obtained in School/College, and offer letters will be issued on first cum first-served basis.

Employment exchange will be responsible to gather a database of students every year from all institutions and segregate and finalize where to place them, instead of students register with an exchange.

Forget Freebies, work to earn and we will give you opportunities to work. Else next generation will suffer

Create more departments in Govt to employ more and more youngsters, maybe the Insurance sector, Mediclaim etc.,

Graduates are hunting for a job and if at all they get it, maybe

placed in a position where they draw around 5000-8000-10000 & 15000 whereas the Daily wages labourers are making more money than these Graduates. Need to regulate

One person from each family has to get a job or business opportunity for sure.

Not more than one person from a family to work in a Government department unless they are selected on a "Merit basis"

CHAPTER ELEVEN

Energy & Power

Every village and town will produce solar energy. Excess energy produced can be sold to the Government for distribution.

No free power to anyone. Of course, for the Farmers and Poor class, it will be supplied at an actual or subsidized cost.

CHAPTER TWELVE

Environment

Avoid transport if it is nearby and can walk. Do not use chemicals at home for cleaning/washing that will eventually reach the water bodies. Soil: Minimize your waste going to landfills. Grow organic food and avoid pesticides/fertilizers. Lead a simple living standard, (everybody has already experienced in a pandemic) consuming very less of resources of any kind. Grow trees only in their natural habitat. Growing trees, and plants in living areas and wasting a lot of fuel and energy to maintain them is wrong.

Throwing garbage only in designated dustbins. Promoting recycling.

Avoid littering as much as possible. Preach cleanliness to your fellow beings.

CHAPTER THIRTEEN

Finance

The top 1% of people have 22% the of income and the remaining 99% of people share 78% of the income.

No more NPA, keep an eye on every account, every bank has to submit a report of large cases that failed to repay on a monthly basis.

Before they declare as NPA, seize all their accounts and take over their company/factory etc., if failed to repay 3 consecutive months and appoint Govt officers on deputation to run the show.

MCA/ROC : for a new company/startup, you have to just apply for company registration, and then you will get

- Certificate of incorporation
- PAN
- TAN
- Import Export Code
- GST
- Startup India Registration
- MSME / Udhyam Registration
- Bank account
-

etc., from one window/one registration.

This is called "ease of doing business"

Income Tax Department

The income tax slabs have to be re-designed in such a way that

1. The more income, the more percentage of Tax to be paid or else spend on the poor in a selected area of your choice.

1. Reasonable percentage for the middle class

3. Remaining people also have to pay a minimum amount as income

Tax which can be anything for example Rs. 100-200 per year (This will be used for the welfare of the same set of people)

IT dept has to certify the nomination papers filed by candidates to contest elections based on their previous income & assets and current income and assets. If there is a huge difference, the same has to be brought to the notice of the concerned Party and Election Commission.

Cricketers, Film stars etc., have to pay MORE as Income Tax which will be spent for Education & development... This amount will be transferred to a Trust which will take care of the poor.

Let everyone come under IT scheme, may pay as low as Rs. 100-200-500-1000 and so on.. These small drops may play a major role in building a New India.

Conduct every year checking/audit of assets and financial status of whole family members of all those who may accumulate wealth to ensure that no unwanted money transactions are being carried out during the previous year.

Corruption has to be eradicated. The highest punishment should be sending the whole family members of a corrupt person to an island, where they have to live the rest of life, working hard to find their bread and butter for themselves. No communication to anyone in the world and no other facility shall be provided to them. The reason for sending the whole family is because everyone in the family enjoys life by using such "bribe" money Hence this punishment to all.

2 paise per (for example) transaction of selling any product or service irrespective of any value, may contribute to the welfare of our fellow citizens. (equally divided by the number of Districts and transferred to every district)

Stop talking about US Dollar ($), we are in India and let's always mention INR instead of USD as and when we talk/write on any figures etc., Those who present anything in USD means they are feeling inferior themselves.

No more tax exemption for anyone in the country, thus generating more revenue for development..

Pension to every senior citizen to meet their minimum commitments.

Every citizen has to pay a nominal charge to the Govt agency for Life Insurance and Mediclaim.

GST

Only 2 slabs of GST

1. All essential items : 05 % *
2. Luxury items : 15 % *

- *** only for example, can be changed based on the revenue model.**

Bring Petrol, Diesel, Gas and related products under GST

One India, One GST Number (Do business in any state, but maintain state-wise data)

CHAPTER FOURTEEN

Food & Public Distribution

Distribute Ration based on Aadhar Card if any of the family member staying away from his/her family, should also get their part of grocery etc.,

In order to follow this practice, all we need to do is to make changes in the Portal regarding all family members and where they are present, based on that if one member is away, the total eligible to the family minus one will go to respective family and that one person will avail the facility anywhere in India as per the data shown.

This will also help the Government to keep the record up to date about the whereabouts of every citizen.

Even for voting purposes he or she is not required to reach their hometown.

Governance

Let everything be transparent to people

Create a department to "Monitor" whether all schemes launched are being properly implemented or not and ensure it reaches all.

Make the transaction of every scheme transparent to our people.

If a person is capable of handling any particular ministry, he/she would be given a chance even if they are in the opposition party.

The core committee in Delhi shall be appointed and they will monitor the activities & growth of each state.

The Prime Minister will visit every Vidhan Sabha once in a year to address and brief them about everything the Indian Government is doing...

The PM candidate will be young, energetic and have a good helping tendency which is in his blood, hence he will surely prove that people have voted, elected and selected the right person.

CHAPTER SIXTEEN

Health & Family Welfare

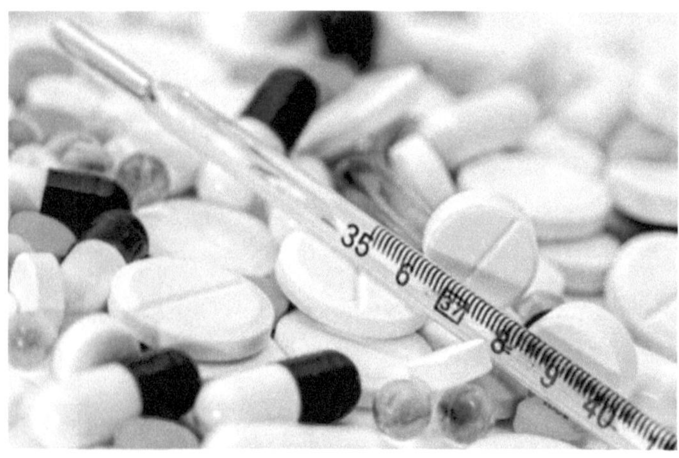

Link all health-related documents, medical history, allergies if any with Blood group etc., with **Aadhar Card**, so that accidents, emergencies if any occurred anywhere, timely attention and first aid can be given to save the precious lives.

Promote Ayurveda, Siddha, our Indian Herbal medicines due to which our earlier generation people lived for a longer period.

Every Indian Citizen shall get assistance from the Government for major treatments through Government Mediclaim or other sources, as "Life is Precious"

Strengthen the Insurance and Mediclaim sector owned by Government to help the people.

Home Affairs

As per my imagination, everyone in Police or any other related security job where their life is under risk and also working hours are very long, irrespective of whatever festival or on any occasion they are away from their home, HAVE TO GET AN INCREASE OF SALARY BY 20 TO 25% TO SHOWCASE GRATITUDE FROM OTHER FELLOW CITIZENS & GOVERNMENT

Nobody can sleep well if they are not there. We need to realize.

In order to bring down Crime and Terrorism, An Mobile APP can be made, where if anyone sees anybody as a suspect can upload details so that the department can take proper action to find out and save from any mishappening. The name of the person reported shall be kept secret.

Increase the strength of the department and allocate duty hours on a shift basis.

Information & Broadcasting

The film industry has to organize a new Award in India called **BASCAR AWARD (BHARATIYA ARTISTIC SOCIETY CULTURAL AWARD & RECOGNITION)** instead of **Oscar** Award & invite all other country films to participate, which has to be ranked number one in the world, through which we can expect more foreigners coming to our country, thereby increasing revenue for our nation.

The ceiling of Salary to film stars etc., to be fixed, in order to control reduced ticket charges at Cinema Halls. Also to avoid multiple crores dumped with less than 1% of the population, which are not in circulation and nor helping the poor.

No highly paid stars will be in Ads. If you want to, then get paid the fixed low remuneration, to ensure the cost of products becomes low. However, most of the stars/ cricketers never use such products which they promote or endorse.

It's better to use common people who really use the products and know the value.

MEDIA

Media will have freedom... will show only facts. If they fail, action will be taken against the concerned Journalist of the media house.

Media personnel (News readers, editors, reporters, cameramen etc.,) to get Insurance. The government will contribute 50% and the remaining by the Press/TV Channel/Media House etc., However, the policy shall be taken only from Government-owned Insurance companies.

The value of the Policy shall be equal for all irrespective of which grade or post they are holding.

CHAPTER NINETEEN

International Affairs

Invite people from other countries through the promotion of Tourism, Culture, and Tradition and participate in Business & Film Awards etc.,

The international relations between our country and other countries have to be very strong to promote successful trade policies and encourage travel-related businesses like tourism, and immigration to people with opportunities.

Allow every nation to cooperate with each other and share the resources if any are required as and when.

Not only the Central Government will work towards building International relations, but even every State in India also has to strengthen international relations on their own, so that together we can collectively make a real **"New India"**

CHAPTER TWENTY

Law & Justice

Courts have to Clear all old cases within 6 months and special courts for new cases & clear within a month. No more dragging of cases by giving date after date. If so, black marks on Judges will affect their careers.

Law must be equal for all irrespective of whether Poor or Rich, as in many cases Rich is given clean chit stating that "Innocent"

Justice is just a name specially in India. If you're rich you're right even if you're wrong. If you have political influence you can get whatever you want. Let's treat everyone equally whether rich or poor.

CHAPTER TWENTY-ONE

MSME

Enter Caption

MSME will focus on manufacturing and set up Trade Agencies in India to sell their products across the Globe and make India the number one manufacturing country in the world.

Providing loans to all MSMEs may be with a minimum amount and enhancement based on repayments status.

The growth of the MSME sector shall be monitored closely and all assistance will be provided to ensure that our Country becomes number one in the world.

Will set up a Factory/Industry in small villages/Town, through which employment opportunities for local candidates, can work without leaving their families.

Create two sections, 1) Manufacturing Sector and 2) Trading & Export so that both can focus on their respective area of work. Through this, we can generate more jobs or entrepreneurs. Thereby revenue goes up.

Set Up a new stock exchange for MSME companies to get listed and grow.

CHAPTER TWENTY-TWO

Rural Development

70% of India's population is in rural areas where Government attention is required, to increase the country's economy, once their productivity increases. This can contribute to "HUGE NUMBERS" to grow our economy.

Make Rural Areas/Villages self-dependent

- Produce Solar Energy

- Rain harvesting
- Setup Clinics with facility
- Small scale units for villagers

Setup Clinics with facilities and Doctors from the nearby town can visit once or twice a week to such clinics, in order to ensure that all villages are covered with Medical facilities and based on requirements they can allocate Doctors accordingly.

Let's identify the basic cause and work on that cause. Normally poverty is due to a lack of employment, which is due to the lack of skill set and awareness. Once it is done, it will improve the economic condition of rural area

Most of the NGOs are functioning only to generate revenue through donations etc., we can take help from those NGOs for planning and implementation of the development of Villages in those districts where NGOs are registered.

Create a village group, where all meet once a week and discuss issues affecting the village, maybe in every Panchayat office. Motivate villagers to maintain the village schools for themselves and also keep a check on teachers for attendance and quality of education etc.,

The urban people are getting all the facilities, but the rural areas are still lagging behind. Large investments are done in the urban areas particularly for delivering education. The rural areas usually lag behind due to a lack of education

They have to go to the cities in order to study further which is more expensive for them and many of them may not afford to do so.

CHAPTER TWENTY-THREE

Science & Technology

Though Science & Technology play a major role and our country is proud to have so many Technical Brains, which are not being used by us for the development of our own country.

We need to utilize them here at ANY COST if we are serious about our growth towards building a powerful nation.

CHAPTER TWENTY-FOUR

Tourism

Design and upload a Portal having information about every destination, tourist spot, Temples, monuments, Culture and many more in one window to attract others to visit India, thereby generating more revenue through money circulation across the nation.

Recruit licensed Guides and Tourist Companies to ensure proper care of people visiting our country.

Take the tourists to rural areas (small villages) and show them the culture, agriculture and tradition etc., so that the economy improves in rural areas too, where small businesses like shops etc., come up.

The heritage, culture and uniqueness of the country are made known to the foreign tourists and the domestic tourists of other parts of India.

Tourism-related infrastructure will expand and generate additional revenues and opportunities for Employment and the Capacities of the local population to acquire new skills and upgrading of the same will result in the development of those areas.

Therefore, let's together try to promote every tourist spot, and place and pull the crowds from other countries.

Transport & Infrastructure

One Vehicle one registration to run within India.

Also one "Pollution Under Control" certificate

No more "Toll" charges on highways or any other roads, as they are built through taxpayer's money and will also be maintained through the recurring revenue of tax.

Youth Affairs & Sports

Government to focus on more facilities in each and every District so that we produce many players and talents from every nook and corner to grab more Awards and recognition at the International level. Though we have talents, they are ignored for not being rich or not having influence to be part of Sports of their interest area.

The ceiling of Salary for crickets and other sports personnel has to be fixed so that we can see a reduction in publicity, and sponsorship costs, which will reflect in the prices of their products/brands.

CHAPTER TWENTY-SEVEN

Political Parties & Politicians

- Any Party found "corrupt" , EC has to Blackmark those candidates and ban them from contesting any election.

- Once people vote and elect a candidate of any party, has no way to sell himself or the voters who have elected, him to any other party unless he or she completes a full-term staying in the same party.

- If they feel like joining another party he/she has to quit the current party and the post held before joining. Accordingly, an election will be held at the particular Assembly / Constituency to re-elect a person.

- Salary will be reduced for MPs/ MLAs and no pension for any politician, as people work for 35 to 40 years to be eligible for pension whereas politicians even if they work for one month get lifetime pension. If they need a pension they are not supposed to call themselves as "Serving the people/country"

- Every time when contestant files nomination papers, his/her assets will be verified by a team and then will be considered to contest an election.(compare with previous ITR/election documents)

- And on completion of their term, again assets will be verified and made public.

- Everyone will get only one chance to contest an election whether you win or lose. Next time the ticket will be given to someone else, not even to any of the blood relations of the previous contestant.

- All personal travel etc., will not be paid for by Govt.

- No telephone bills for personal use at residents for MPs

- Recurring expenditure of each MLA/MP/MINISTER has to be uploaded on a website and made transparent to everyone.
- Avoid spending on visits when not required and stay connected online. Make it both way communication, so that you can listen to others' Mann ki Baat too.

Once a month, MLA/MP along with all officers from different departments will meet the people of respective constituencies to hear their grievances and ensure it is resolved by the next meeting.

- No more "Kurtas"
- No more "Netas"
- Only Professionals to run the country

- Any individual can contest only once and allow others next time.

Cast, Religion less society No reservation seats in any assembly or constituency for a person to contest in an elections Make Laws very strict on corruption and on criminal cases Speaker in the parliament and state assemblies should be replaced with bureaucrats and not a politician.

CHAPTER TWENTY-EIGHT

General

One ID only (smart card) with all info like Aadhar, Driving License, Ration, Voter, Health info etc.,

Using "Public convenience" will become completely FREE for all.

Transportation (Bus, Train, Flight) at 50% cost for all senior citizens irrespective of travelling to any state within the country.

Educational and Health-related services will be provided at a very low cost.

No Free items. But will provide many essentials at a subsidized cost

Each assembly constituency will have people-friendly centers to assist you to avail every scheme announced by Govt. Concerned District Collectors will be responsible for the same.

National Awards like Padmashri etc., will be given to people like Kisan / Farmers, Coolie, Auto / Taxi Drivers, Cleaning department, Medical Staff, social workers who help or save people etc.,

Nowhere in any certificate Caste / Religion will be mandatory. we are all one. Our religion and caste is INDIAN.

Contribute ?10 each for any mishappening, from the District level as and when required. **People helping People**. (Helping yourselves)

All the work done by Government contractors in your area has to be verified and approved by a team of local people for payments.

Anyone found wrong, their degree will be cancelled & banned from doing their respective job/profession.

Female: Stop posing nude pics and posting on social media. Else, the person in the pic and who uploads the same shall be punished severely for encouraging crime in society.

All contract staff will become permanent

718 districts can be adopted by Rich, Industrial, celebrity, and Corporate companies, each district can be adopted by few people/companies. Even NRIs may also consider this option. They will get Tax benefits. If any individual or a Corporate company wants to adopt more areas are welcome.

HOW IT SHOULD WORK :

- Can hire the poor and feed them
- Hire local people for any work within the area like Road construction etc.,
- Setup small industries for them to work
- In case of natural calamity, take care of people in your specific area
- Install Solar Panels / Lights with your brand publicity for free
- Help the poor in education
- Setup small clinics with the medical facility

If anyone violates rules example: traffic rule: They cannot escape by paying money/fine, whoever is in that vehicle, all of them have to work in any nearby project, maybe road construction for one day free of cost.

No more just disaster management, instead it will be "Pre-disaster management" as things will be planned to face any kind of national calamity.

Invite youngsters from each village to set up a business to feed the entire village.

Will fix Ceiling for individuals to keep money and excess amount if found will be seized for development purpose.

CHAPTER TWENTY-NINE

Conclusion

- Choose only person/s from the same area/field of having the expertise to become a concerned Minister

- Strict Policy & Punishment will surely help us to have clean Ministers, MPs, MLAs and so on...

- All Government agencies, departments, and the judicial system will be functioning properly and no need to dance the way politicians ask them to do so..

- Election process will be perfect and will set an example for the rest of the world.

- Production of Rice, wheat, spices, fruits and vegetables will increase though we may expect more revenue from the export of surplus

- Retain Culture, Tradition and transfer them from Generation to Generation and save them before completely destroyed

- No more homework for Children during summer vacation

- Sudden improvement and reasonable growth can be seen in Information Technology and communication as experts will be driving the ministry

- Productivity might increase in the Defence sector as their spare time will be utilized properly for the production of various goods they need for themselves.

- New education system will enlighten and brighten the students to think of various innovative ideas and implement them, resulting in the growth of the country.

- More and more employment opportunities shall be created while making new entrepreneurs who will in turn accommodate more employees. The introduction of more Government departments, also helps the people to join, thereby can remove the word "unemployment" from the Indian Dictionary.

- The Energy and Power sector will help us to avoid pollution and increase the generation of energy through the Solar system.

- Keeping the environment neat and clean to breathe pure air

- Finance may play a major role in generating more revenue than ever before through Income Tax, GST etc, Banks will see more transactions from the MSME sector and we will witness "Ease of doing business" in reality.

- Food (Ration) distribution to all shall be streamlined to help the people.

- Actual "Governance" can be seen by everyone, as it will be **completely transparent and not just talking about numbers & figures, it will be shown publicly and will be done by the people and not by the Government**. Every scheme will be monitored and ensure that they are implemented on a regular basis.

- Good Health of all shall be the responsibility of our Government, to assist whenever people need it, and it will be the responsibility of people to pay taxes on time to the Government.

- Police and related security agencies/departments shall get an increased salary package, to ensure efficient and hard work.

- By introducing **BASCAR** Award, we will be more powerful than any other country. Also shall generate more revenue, thereby new business houses may take birth, meaning more money in circulation.

- Advertisements using newcomers and actual users of the products can help to see a reduction in the prices of various products.

- Media will be given free hand to showcase only facts and figures and no need to manipulate anything or favour a particular individual or any political party. They are assured of an Insurance policy, being in a position where a threat is common in their everyday life.

- Need to maintain good relationships with international organizations and other countries by inviting them to visit India, having various natural spots in different states

- Law & Orders will be our prime focus and hence not to worry about dragging the cases for a lifetime. We'll work towards the "Case and Close" way.

- MSME sector shall grow faster, thereby increasing manpower, production of goods and trade activities can take our country to a great height.

- Rural Area: Villages may not be called Villages more in the near future as they will be converted into a Mini Towns by providing adequate infrastructure and other facilities, while they are being made "Self Dependent"

- Increase Tourists from international, while inviting domestic tourists from each other countries within India to increase cash flow throughout India.

- We are living in India which we call "One India", so let's have One Registration, One Pollution Certificate and One time Road Tax in the country and remove "Toll" charges forever, as the roads are built and maintained by Taxpayer money and why pay Toll? It's like "Paying Rent for our own House"

- We can have various sports complexes/facilities in every district to encourage youngsters to practice and win, irrespective of whether they are rich or influenced, go only by talent.

- No politician can contest or serve more than one term and also no other person in his/her family will be allowed to contest any election. Thus, others from the same area, assembly, and constituency get a chance to be part of serving the nation.

- National Awards to even small workers like Sweepers, Medical Ward Boys etc., not just to celebrity, sportsmen and Rich

- Pension to politicians for serving the people will be withdrawn as they are not working, they are serving.

- Once elected by people, they have to complete their term in the same party and at any cost, they are not allowed to switch over to another party, as voters choose him/her for a particular party and they do not have any rights to do anything on their own without consulting their voters.

- On completion of one term, they are not allowed to contest any election including their immediate family members and will give chance to others who are working hard for the party or the society.

It's A Beginning Of New India

I am not against any party or any individual, actually against the system and the way we run the country.

Given a chance to run the Government, we can form a team of professionals from different fields and assure you that we will make India A POWERFUL COUNTRY IN THE WORLD

Thus, I have created a New India which is purely an imagination. If people unite together, imagination can be converted into reality.

Will you?